PAINT ME LIKE I AM

PAINT ME LIKE I AM

TEEN POEMS FROM WRITERSCORPS

HarperTempest

An Imprint of HarperCollins*Publishers*

Paint Me Like I Am

Copyright © 2003 by WritersCorps

Library of Congress Cataloging-in-Publication Data
Paint me like I am : teen poems from WritersCorps.—1st HarperTempest ed.
p. cm.
ISBN 0-06-447264-7 (pbk.) — ISBN 0-06-029288-1 (lib. bdg.)
1. Teenagers' writings, American. 2. Teenagers—Poetry.
I. WritersCorps.
PS591.T45 P358 2003   2002005942
811'.60809283—dc21   CIP
                                                                  AC

Typography by Andrea Vandergrift
❖

First HarperTempest edition, 2003
Visit us on the World Wide Web!
www.harpertempest.com

Table of Contents

Foreword
by Nikki Giovanni

I know this   it is difficult to grow up
it always was
it always will be

I know this   nobody can tell you how to do it
You just make the same mistakes and
You just thrill to the same excitement

I know this   Life is a good idea

I think   it is illogical to assume there is no other
life in the Universe
I think   the possibility of re-creating ourselves is
in our hands
we just happen to be the only species that
we respect
It is our loss.
We need   to listen to those who are forming
We need   to hear the cry of those in pain
We need   to respect the fear and embrace the longing
of those who are new to the wilderness

I know   imagination is a good idea

I know	those forging forward must embrace creativity
I know	humans will shrivel from emotional needs
	before we die of starvation or dehydration
	The body will take care of itself.

We need food for the Soul

        We need poetry . . . We deserve poetry

We owe it to ourselves to re-create ourselves

        And find a different if not better way to live

Paint Me Hopeful   Paint Me Futuristic   Paint Me Nikki
        I'm a Poet

One of the most celebrated poets of our time, Nikki Giovanni has long been associated with WritersCorps. Ms. Giovanni has been honored with numerous awards, including the Langston Hughes Award for Distinguished Contribution to Arts and Letters and the NAACP Image Award for Literature. She grew up in Knoxville, Tennesee, and Cincinnati, Ohio, and attended

Fisk University. Two of her best-known books for young readers are *Spin a Soft Black Song* and *Ego-Tripping and Other Poems for Young Readers*. She is currently University Distinguished Professor at Virginia Tech.

The Artists

"Breathe in experience, breathe out poetry."
—Muriel Rukeyser

The Writing Journal

Begin with a blank black-and-white composition notebook. Make it yours by covering it with pictures, symbols, colored lettering, and words that reflect your own personality. This is the beginning of your personal writing journal.

Paint Me Like I Am

Why don't you paint me
Like I am?
Paint me happy,
Laughing, running down a path of happiness
Paint me with a smile on my face.

Paint me with long wavy black hair
And my rosy cheeks.
Paint me sunflowers, red and white roses.
Paint me with bears, rabbits and baby deer
In my arms, dancing around me.
Paint me somewhere wonderful
Somewhere where there's sunshine and
A light blue sky
With butterflies floating
Around that lovely sky.

Paint me without my sadness.
Paint me without my sorrow.
Paint me without my tears.
Paint me so my pain won't show.

Can you see the face telling you paint me happy,
Paint me with life, but most of all
Paint me free.

Delia Garcia *San Francisco*

The Artists

Two African American guys:
One is tall with white hair,
Smoking a cigarette,
The other is smaller,
 But strong,
With white pants and black shoes.

They stand on plastic boxes
In a dark, dirty alley surrounded by trash,
Newspapers and broken glass,
Rotting food like fish and chicken bones
All mixed together with gray rats running through
Looking for food.

The young men don't pay attention to these things.

They're just painting
Themselves
On the old wooden walls
Next to the fire escape stairs.

Their only friends
Are the quiet night
And the beautiful moon.

Kenny Zapeda *San Francisco*

What I See Daydreaming

Looking into the chalkboard,
It looks like someone just erased it.
But to me it looks like a dragon with spikes
Pushing their way out of the dragon's body.
If you move your head,
It looks like a fish pond.
If you blink your eyes fast,
It's an elephant.

Sarah Villeda-Holmes *San Francisco*

Keys

To have a key
Is to open up doors,
Open your imagination.
Let your thoughts run wildly through the
Dark crisp night.
Chant words and phrases over and over
Until you are delirious.

Adaya Brand-Thomas *San Francisco*

My Poem

My poem can fight,
My poem can sing,
My poem can fly,
But it has no wings.

My poem can wake
You up from your sleep,
My poem can rhyme,
And stick to the beat.

My poem can give,
My poem can take,
My poem can tell
The real from the fake.

My poem can see,
My poem makes you read,
My poem isn't food,
But it does fill a need.

Krystal White *Washington, D.C.*

Jazz Feels

Jazz makes me feel relaxed and sleepy,
It's like a lightning bolt of peace,
It has the power to hold me in its musical grip,
With a mystic, fast-and-slow-together sound.
Jazz is like a long-lasting dream-sound
In your head, and you never want it to go away.
I seek the hidden answers in the music,
The rhythm is curved and tender,
It feels like I open a door
And step into a jazz zone,
That makes me feel alive,
In my dreams,
Relaxed
And sleepy.

Michael Toomer *Washington, D.C.*

Hip-Hop Shoes

Hip-hop shoes've been everywhere,
Hip-hop shoes make people stare;
Hip-hop shoes sing the blues,
Hip-hop shoes are not for fools.

Hip-hop shoes dance night and day,
Hip-hop shoes go out to play;
Hip-hop shoes step to the beat,
Hip-hop shoes are on your feet.

Hip-hop shoes are in style,
Hip-hop shoes make people smile;
Hip-hop shoes are smooth and quick,
Hip-hop shoes always fit.

Hip-hop shoes go 'round the world,
Hip-hop shoes get all the girls;
Hip-hop shoes fly through the air
Hip-hop shoes are on the feet of the mayor.

Hip-hop shoes I love to wear,
Hip-hop shoes, I have a pair;
Hip-hop shoes, mine, all mine,
Hip-hop shoes send shivers down my spine.

Bernard Best *Washington, D.C.*

Paint Me

Paint me Black. Paint me.

Me, Black, the most authentic thing you can see.

Paint me Black 'cause I don't want anything to change
my shade.

Immerse my soul in its essence and show me what you've
made.

Splash the most beautiful tones upon my skin.

Paint me Black for the person within.

Paint me Black. Paint me

For all that I am for my history.

Paint me and shine me up for the world to know.

Paint me Black 'cause I've got stories other colors haven't
told.

Paint me Black and I'm sure you'll find

The other color fits me perfect, but doesn't control the
mind.

Natriece Laynette Spicer *San Francisco*

Friendship

> *"Don't bother just to be better than your contemporaries or predecessors. Try to be better than yourself."*
>
> —*William Faulkner*

14

**Write as if you were your favorite month or the
month your birthday is in.**

Say you pick October. How does October feel? What is the color
of October? What does October say? What does October eat?
What do you hate about being October? Does October sleep,
dance, sing?

15

You Were Fine Till I Met Your Mind

"Oh look at him. Now I like something like that."

6'1", gray eyes, slender, the cutest face
I have ever seen
"Hey you! Yeah, what is your name?"
And when he replied it was like
"Whhuuttttt!"
What happened! What up with that?
"and what school do you go to?"
when he answered it was like
huhhhh
I mean . . . damn!!!
"and what district is that?"
and he didn't know!
Okay, it's like damn another one?
Why the cute ones gotta turn out to be
The dumb ones (No offense)
But seriously, what have y'all been on over
The years to make y'all like that?

You have the face
But not the brains

You have the eyes
But not the heart

You have the body
But not the confidence

Now, it's like "Okay, nice talkin to ya."
And send you on your way.
But it's nice outside, a so-called "nice day"
When I met a boy who turned out to be slow!
And it could be anyone,
It could be you, you, or you . . .
And that's why
In this world
It makes love harder and harder to

Find

Tinea Plummer *Bronx, New York*

For John

I wanted to
Write a poem
That rhymes
But revolution
Doesn't lend
Itself to be
Bopping

Then my family
Who thinks I hate
Asked do you ever
Write tree poems
I like trees so I
Thought I'll write
A beautiful green
Tree poem
Peeked out
My window to check
The yard was covered
With concrete no
Green no trees grow
In the Bronx
Then, well I thought

The sky I'll do a big
Blue sky poem but
All the clouds have
Winged low since
It was elected
So I thought again
And it occurred
To me
Maybe I shouldn't
Write at all but
Then I remember you
& I realize
That these are
Poetic times.

Joyanna Deluna *Bronx, New York*

I Know

I know you would not want me
If I danced without my veil
I know you would not see me
If in light's embrace I lie
But that night,
As your hands fingered my hips
And my lips fondled your eyelids
You found me in my purest form
And you craved me

You craved me.

Tabia Brown *Bronx, New York*

Friendship

Since the days when the Now & Laters melted in our
     pockets
I hate friendship
We be together every day
Chino Suarez is my best friend
Friendship makes me think how
Y'all been my peoples; had my back
You think you my friend? I thought so, too
You've been my friend
I mean cuz there's too many two-faces
Chillin and doin shit we ain't supposed to
If we got to throw down we gonna throw down
I would have been alone all my life
Never had friends like this
But a friend doesn't two-face you
My back-up, my confidant, my partner in crime
You don't really know who to trust
Trying to be big boys, trying to run shit
We talk about shit we can't even tell our moms about
If I didn't have a friend
Like fam, yo, for real, for life
A friend doesn't steal from you and lie to you
And even when things got rough

I only have one true friend
Acting like we hard when we really not
But we boys so we talk to each other
A boy, a dog, a nigga
Better than family cuz we ain't had ta rock together
You ain't my best friend or friend
Your laugh we there
Even that's not what I call friendship
But you know why/cause we boys to the end, dogs
And that's my idea of friendship
Maybe a girlfriend
We chose ta rock together, you know
But we still peoples
To smooth things out

23   Sarah Jones, Joseph Roldan, Chino Suarez, Taraun Morene,
Terrence Banks, John Rodriguez, Sarah Lydia Chaleman
Bronx, New York

Her Eyes

Her eyes are as beautiful as the sky
When I look into them I think about
The blue sky over us. I like the way
She moves them the way she rolls
Them at the people who got beef with her
I like her eyes that look like the blue sky.

Joseph Arias *Bronx, New York*

Untitled

Bodies sprawled along the shelter's floor—
Like sloppy cursive writing
Like a herd of forgotten cattle we sit
Chewing on the cud of our precious memories
In my mind's eye I see you, Nate
Your silken hair which tumbled
And rustled in the wind—
Tendrils like beckoning fingers
Your eyes the color of pastures green
In which the good Lord made me down to lie
I remember the rough, linen texture of your worn jacket—
The sheet upon the luxurious bed
That was your shoulder
How poor is this tiled floor by comparison!
I lost you so many addictions ago
Now, on the floor of this pit
With nothing but hope to light my way,
I part the cloud of my sins
And spend the night
Ensconced in the warm embrace of your memory

Anna Sproul *Washington, D.C.*

Nothing But the Blues

I've been happy baby.
Ever since you died.
I've been rich baby.
Ever since you died.
I belong to nothing but the blues.
Baby, how blue can you get?

I wanted to invest my money.
But you said, "Oh no!"
I said I want to save my money.
You said, "I want to go to the show."
I said you're being dumb.
You said, "I'm having fun."

I saw you spend it on drugs instead.
And now you're dead.
I'm rich, baby.
Ever since you died.
I been having nothing but the blues.
Baby, how blue can you get?

Byron X. Miller *Washington, D.C.*

Forever Left Nothing Underneath Me

Forever left nothing underneath me.
No more letters about things
That open doors so you, purple plant,
Ring in doors, bang money
For time left broke.
Flying oceans apart, feet begin
Swelling. Drought,
Run, hide. Inside darkness moans
Like aliens. Rain would travel
Without boats.

They say ice brings cold mouth
Water melts popsicles, slippery
Mildew and fiery stains alarm
With total singing.
Shoelaces tangle my fingers.
Love believes something no one understands
When midnight hears.
Alone.
Shoestring romance triangles friendship
Longing for the right tunnel to fasten happiness,
Cry loudly above streetlight, cars, winds, horns

Around barn life because yesterday is
Disappearing from view.
Windows dream pictures painted oil and always.
Green steps find forever.

Tiana, Chipu, Aja, Colette *San Francisco*

Untitled

Blackberry Molasses is what I thought about
        As I look into her eyes
        As I stared beyond his glasses
            Solid knowledge
            So surprised my mind
                My thoughts roamed
As smoke
                        Freely

Making me feel at home
        I seemed to gain knowledge by listening
        To his words
            The memory of her face
        Not body
        Made me think of feelings
Not heard in his words

A Star

Emotional recollections lead to
Central Avenue Blues
I am the true vine of spicy life bright nite
Connecting your veins
Pumping
Magenta chakra
To your impulses
Let's go to N.Y.
For a love supreme
I've fallen for dreams
And we can never be separated
Triumph in Paris
Let it be known
Penetrating normal levels of thought
Across the globe
Spoiled memories
Left out too long I think or
Maybe they weren't consumed fast enough for the speed
    of negativity
Regal white tiger
Ghost of the renaissance
Her essence washed away from cleaning up behind
Drips of red wine intoxications and cloudy smoke
Foggy to the distinction of what's real &

Actually happening to her crumbling life
Purple moons of woman scent
Bursting in reaction to beautiful stone
As you reminisce you sit alone
Transporting yourself to a time when you didn't need
    drugs to feel high my oh my
What a lovely life
I used to be a star—beauty, charm, elegance
A gift
Staring through the mirror
I become familiar with an unknown reflection
I struggle to find traces of what used to be there
I look down ashamed
Find traces of heroin embedded in gray arms
A reminder of her last affair
An emotional recollection
A love supreme

Lauren Wyatt *Washington, D.C.*

I Too Am America

"There is a vitality, a life force, an energy, a quickening that is translated through you into action and because there is only one of you in all of time this expression is unique. . . . It is your business to keep it yours, clearly and directly, to keep the channel open."

—Martha Graham

Find portraits (on postcards or from magazines) of a variety of faces.

Choose one that interests you.

Write a poem from this person's point of view. Imagine how this person sees the world.

I Too Am America

I too am America.

I am the tools that bang
To make all your buildings and factories
That pollute the cities.

I am the people not mentioned
In your stories of the war.

I am in the words you speak
But still you don't mention my people.

America is made of the people that work the
Hardest.
The rich people think we're on the bottom,
But really we're on top.

All the rich people want is to spend and spend.

I am the bodies that take pesticides all day
But still no pay!

I am the arms and legs of children
That make your expensive shoes
And still we lose!

I am the people that get beat down every day
In Philly and L.A.
For what we look like not for what we did.

But when you do this,
All we do is get stronger and stronger
And beat you the right way
Not the wrong way.
I will beat you with my words
And not your violence.

I too am America!

Chris McMahon *San Francisco*

Two Histories

Daddy wanted to name me Wilhemina after his mother.
You know you're supposed to name your baby after
    someone who's gone,
Not alive.
But then my mother protested.
I should carry her mother's name, Anne.
"Rachel" kept me from the arguments and sour family
    disputes,
But did it compromise or anger both sides?
And that's what I'm stuck with,
Every day
Every move
I'm a compromise
Light skin
But thick bone structure
Half 'n' half Jewish girl who fights for BSU* unity
Latke and greens
The horah and the butterfly
Act White
Won't date Black men
Thinks she's better
Has good hair
Looks more Latina than half-breed
But that boy always called me mixed in such an ugly way

Some say, "Nigga get off the swing"
Others say, "You're really not like those other Black
    people"
And I get told it's better to pretend I'm White
But I got two histories in me
Both enslaved
And both warriors.

*Black Student Union

Rachel Stephanie Bolden-Kramer *San Francisco*

Good Night Petals

I'm a sleepy flower
And the ground waves at me,
The pollen stings my tongue.
Megan Cordella steps on me.
She's on her way to Kevin's house.
The ground's not waving,
And I'm no flower.
She treats me as a rock on the ground.
The dirt suddenly discovers my nose.
I ain't hanging around here no more.
The ground's wet so it rains.
"And all the perfumes of Arabia
Will not sweeten this little hand!"
And I fly toward the sky.
The clouds say "Hello."
Ellimay knows me.
She sees me.
And tomorrow I have no petals.
My head is not completely with my heart.
I tell only true lies.
The true dreams of Nazareth
Bring me to weeping petals.
Even though I'm not a flower,

I hear the rainbow I make up.
I'm an iota in that rainbow
And I'm on my way.
Good-bye ground, good night petals.

Ellen Donnelly *Washington, D.C.*

Why

Why don't somebody
Anybody
Ask me what no one dares to ask
Like
What I feel
What I want
What I need
Who I am today
Who I will be tomorrow
I want people to ask
To say hi when I pass by
To sit and talk to me
I need to tell people what I think
Need a girlfriend to share things with
When I need fun
When I need help
People think I'm a nobody
I'm really the queen of happiness
Just sometimes I'm not nice
If somebody
Anybody
Asked me
What no one dares to ask
They would know.

Tommi Jones *Washington, D.C.*

I Am the Woman You Should Fear

I am the woman you should fear
I am the epitome of goals
The summary of aspirations
When knocked down
I rise with resolution
Not only for myself
But for my people.

I am the woman you should fear
So don't walk through my neighborhood at night
Cause I'll hit you with spoken truth
When my vibes already had you shook—
Shook cause I walk with my head high
Unlike the slide you had five minutes ago.
Yeah though I didn't realize when you and
Your boys beat her off the block cause she
Wouldn't let y'all run a train
Yeah well this train runs express.

I am the woman who pays her own way.
I am the woman who is self-reliant.
I am the woman who is independent.

When I speak my shhhhhh
It's not your money
I'm after
It's you
Your game might be tight but mine has
No circulation running through it.
I'm sneaky like a snake, yet shy like a koala bear
I'm little like a mouse, yet powerful like a lion
I'm pretty but this shhhh, it can get ugly.
So be careful and watch what you say
Because my mentality level skyrocketed
To the moon years ago
But this is only a premonition of
What you're up against
I suggest
Inquire before you battle
SCARED YET?

Marsha Goshine ("Scotch Tape") *Bronx, New York*

My Real Name

Today my name is colorful.
Yesterday my name was dead souls.
Tomorrow my name will be lively spirits.
My friends think my name is fire.
The police think my name is burden.
My parents think my name is symphony.
Secretly I know my name is anything
I want it to be.

Elena Noel *Washington, D.C.*

I Am

I am
A transcendent light
Alive and fighting, in an unforgiving life
Graceful in execution
Undulating in thought
A tempestuous soul
Bravely riding the ins and outs
Ups and downs
Outsides and insides
Over and aboves
Of emotions, dreams and love
Darkness encircles, but
Intelligence bright
On a smiling face
Capricious in nature
Definitive in thought
Beautiful, in love
You are
Ensconced in layers of
Salvation Army clothes
Protected against a capricious, biting cold
An unforgiving memory
Worms its way, unwilling, into

The very seams of your coat
A single down feather escapes
From this tiny fissure
And drops, gently
Unaware of the tempest
That has released it
Beautiful, graceful
It floats to the ground, undulating, mesmerizing
No longer transcendent, no longer
Symbolic
You see it painfully, as your eyes squeeze
Shut
Against the bright glare of the sun.

Alaya Robinson *Washington, D.C.*

I Am a Shadow

What kind of name is Helen? Simple, boring, practical and plain. I'm not Helen. I'm unique. I'm original. I'm creative and bold. I follow you in the morning. You follow me in the evening. I creep. You can't get away from me unless you like darkness. Where there's light, there's me. I'm behind you, in front of you, below you, I follow you. I am not Helen. I am a shadow. A dark, mysterious image of you. I can't be heard, I can't be touched, I can't be smelled, I can't be tasted. I can be seen. I can be understood. You can step on me, jump on me, throw things at me, I will not get hurt. I am a shadow.

Eyes of Arabian Skies

My eyes look like the Arabian skies at night.
And sometimes they are the beauty of the land,
The diamonds of night.
My eyes are tigers' roars and leopard skin.
They are sky and oceans on fire.
My eyes tell me how to play the flying flute
And to see my sunken sea.
They grow like pine trees.
Sometimes they spy.

Sadaf Minapara *San Francisco*

Where I Come From

I come from a long line of
Confusion,
A long line of
Patience
And understanding myself
When there's no one who understands.
I come from
A long line
That never ends
But bends
To the right
And then to the left.
I come from a long line of
Liars
And fakers,
A line of cutters
Who step in front of me
In line
In a long line
Where I come from.

Jennifer Robles *San Francisco*

My Soul

Sometimes
When I feel like I'm going to fall apart
I hold my ribs, all the way around,
Both sides.
My ribs hold me together,
Like glue.
They keep my breath close to my heartbeat.
They keep my soul from escaping and
Leaving me, grounded.
I hold brightness and shadows in
The hollow where my ribs meet.
I hold them there in the memories
Of slow, sorrowful music and
Porch steps.
I hold my ribs, until I feel solid.
Until my legs are tree trunks and
My fingers are fruit.

Ember Ward *San Francisco*

Moe

My name is Moevasa
It means sleeping ocean
Restless nights on the moving sea.
Friends call me Moe.
Not moe money, or
Moe better blues
But just moe . . .
Moe loves you you can say.
My family says Moevasa
To its fullest.
They want the whole truth,
Not just half a truth.
It's important, they believe
To pass on the baton.
I guess so.

Moevasa Sagapelutell *San Francisco*

Race

Race
People hate for it
Talk shit for it
Get arrested for it
Die in burning churches for it

Mamas pray for it
Cry for it
Love for it
Fight for it
Men in white sheets kill for it
Little girls wish their eyes were blue for it
Some try to convince themselves that
It does not affect them for it
Mirrors show disgrace for it
Fuck you for it
Wanting for it
Boys from Chicago get killed for saying hey
Baby for it
Liquor stores appear on every corner for it
Crack infiltrates whole communities for it
Billie Holiday sings about strange fruit for it
No matter how much it is thought of as
Nonexistent

It will never leave us
It flows in our society like a never-ending river,
It beats people down slowly
And appears through the crack in the sidewalk.

We can try to hide it
To convince ourselves that it has disappeared
But in reality
Race is immortal

Gemma Mirkensen *San Francisco*

Keeper of Blue Sand

I am the keeper
Of the sand
The color sky blue
It's a job I take
Pride in
People ask me why do I have
A fascination with
Sky blue sand
I simply say it's
Time in a bottle
It spreads where
The wind takes it
And lands
All over the place

Why is the sand
Sky blue people
Wanna know
I say it's the color
Of the sky
The color of life
It spreads around

Never stays in
One place

I am the keeper
Of sky blue sand
I tell people sand
Has many meanings
A heart sinking never
Coming up or like
Time sinking away
I am still and will
Always be the keeper
Of sky blue sand

Felicia Marable *Bronx, New York*

Why I Write Poetry

by Kevin Powell

I have not always been a fan of poetry. Nah. In fact, I hated it and thought poetry an activity for the overly sensitive—and suckers. Suckers in the sense that I, a Black boy from the ghetto, would—could—never let my guard down long enough for you, the observer, to see me—naked—as I am. But the reality is that I had always, on the down low, dug poetry, be it the sensual sonnets of William Shakespeare, the dark meditations of Edgar Allan Poe, or the lonesome thoughts of Emily Dickinson.

However, it was not until I encountered the first very traumatic experience of my adult life, at age twenty-two, that poetry really began to mean something to me. You see, I was suspended from my university for an indiscretion I will not share here. Having been the first person in my immediate family to attend college, I was devastated and could not tell my moms what had happened. Between sudden bouts with insomnia and school-mandated trips to a therapist, I scrawled words which became stanzas which became my initial attempts at poetry. Although I had studied this literary form in both high school and college, I did not know if poems were supposed to be long or short, if they should rhyme or not, nor if what I was writing was actually good or not.

Back then I did not care, to be honest. I had wanted to be a writer since I was eleven and, outside of some short fiction I penned during my high school years, this post-college writing was the first time I felt free—and truly felt that I was, indeed, a writer. And how amazing it was, yo. To be able to say whatever I wanted, to push the door to my imagination and walk through, without fear, to those spaces I never knew existed.

And it was not enough for me to write poetry in isolation. I knew I had to share my words with other people and I soon found myself in hole-in-the-wall spots in north Jersey and New York City, reading to audiences of maybe ten people. I was mad happy about that too. I felt empowered, that my voice, my life, my world, mattered. That poetry was, no doubt, special, magical, a gift from some greater being and I was merely the vessel carrying the word.

It took me a few years but I eventually recovered from that college suspension. Now all these years later, after five books, numerous magazine and newspaper articles, and travels across America and outside of the States to places like England, France, and the Caribbean, I cannot help but think back to those very innocent days when I kept a tiny notepad in my back pocket and tried to capture everything I felt at any given moment, on the subway, at a grocery store, while walking down a street in Newark, or Harlem, or Brooklyn.

Today I cannot picture what it would be like not being a poet. Yeah, I am sensitive, because one cannot be a poet without having some level of sensitivity. Without some connection to one's soul, and the souls of other human beings. And, yeah, I am a sucker, for words. For sure, I love words and the poetry made from stringing just the right words together. It is this coming together of pen and paper, of fingers and computer keys, of raw-dog emotions and instant testimonies that make poetry—to me—as necessary as the blood beating a path to our hearts.

The New York City-based **Kevin Powell** is a poet, journalist, essayist, activist, and public speaker. Kevin is the author of five books, including his editorship of the recent HarperCollins release *Who Shot Ya? Three Decades of Hiphop Photography* (images by Ernie Paniccioli), which is the first-ever pictorial history of hiphop. Kevin's essays, articles, and reviews have appeared in many publications, including the *Washington Post*, *Essence*, *Newsweek*, and *Vibe*, where he was a longtime staff writer. A highly sought-after political and pop cultural commentator, Kevin has shared his views on VH1, BET, CNN, and a host of other media outlets. And Kevin first reached the national spotlight as a cast member on the original season of MTV's *The Real World*, the most successful reality-based program in television history.

As We Sit Here

*"What you are shrieks so loudly I cannot
hear what you say."*
—Ralph Waldo Emerson

Imagine yourself sitting in a room that holds everybody who has ever been a part of your family.

See yourself looking around the room, noticing facial features, body types. Who smiles with their hands covering their mouths? How does each one walk and dance? What do you have in common with these people?

Diary of an Abusive Stepfather

Wednesday, it's 6 A.M.
It's 7 hours from the happy one,
So I have to deal with drinking beer
And having to deal with you, my bastard son,
Your mother that stupid bitch, she doesn't help,
Pick that shit up before I hit you with the fucking belt
You're pathetic every day you get dumber and dumber,
The only reason you're here is cause I had no rubber,
I despise you I don't even know why I try to help my
Family when "You" make me go back to the bottle,
The only reason I drink is cause you get me stressed,
How you used to cry and make a fucking mess,
I hated the day you were put on this earth,
That's why I told the doctor I'm not your dad
Just a friend of your mom before birth,
You're a bastard!
Did you hear what the fuck I said?
Now wipe that up before I hit you
Across your fucking head!
Don't forget to pick my clothes up from off the floor,
Don't you hear that dumb ass?
Get it—it's the fucking door!
Who's that?

ACS?
Who they here for, me?
What they got a problem with me
Beating you since you were 3?
They also say you haven't gone
To school in quite a while
What do they know?
They can't tell me shit, you're my child!

67   **Jayson Tirado** *Bronx, New York*

Diary of an Abused Son

Stop it Dad!
I'm tired of you screaming and yelling!
And for god's sake stop hitting me
Don't you know I'm eleven
You brought me here I didn't ask to be,
If you had any heart you'd stop drinking
And take care of me,
I'm tired of the beatings!
You attack me for no reason!
It didn't matter what time
It didn't matter what season,
In the heat or the cold,
And I bet you thought that no one knows,
And guess what, contrary to what you know,
I did tell someone,
Some guy on the phone, his number's 9-1-1
Now I bet I won't be picking up
Your shit any more,
But where you're going, forget your clothes,
Don't drop the soap on the floor,
Now you're in a 10 x 12 all by yourself,
All because you lost your temper
And started using a belt.

Jayson Tirado *Bronx, New York*

Papá

It seems as though
We had lost our touch
Are we getting it back?

We were so close years ago
When I was younger
We were like little kids
Always trying something new
Even the things we knew would get us in trouble
With Mom
As the years progressed
Our relationship started tearing
And wearing out

You saw me changing
But did not enjoy acknowledging it
Did you not know I could change?
That my branches would stem out?
Well, they have
Take these flowers I offer you
Whose seeds are yours

Marcela Ferlito *Washington, D.C.*

Tide

When the world ends,
I will be sitting on a beach
Watching the tide come in
With my mother,
Sharing an ice cream sundae
With hot fudge.
I will be skipping
Smooth
Flat
Rocks
Across the ocean's current,
Enjoying life
For the time at last.
Mother and I will remember
The good times
And
Look at old photo albums.
I will
Cry for the
Time that will
Not be and dream of it
When the world ends.

Leia Hayhoe *Washington, D.C.*

Sister

The night rides up like a newborn child.
Her eyes see me as my eyes see her.
Her hands feel like soft tissue.
Her soft beautiful hair feels
Like a yellow blanket on the bed.
I see her in my dream.
I put her to bed and she falls to sleep
As I sing to her through the night.
I see her grow up.
Only that little baby sister
I love more than the world.

Teyonna Phillips *Washington, D.C.*

He Is Only Two

As the sun rises in the east
And its rays just barely touch the blinds
He is already looking at me
I can tell he wants to stroke
My face
But he doesn't want to wake me
He somehow manages to slither
Like a rattlesnake
Onto my bed to lie beside me
Then as I peek through my eyelids
I see him staring at me
His arm around my neck
And the tip of his nose touching mine
His eyes seem to be pleading

He calls my name
So I wake up
He knows it is tomorrow
And now promises
Made yesterday
Of ice cream and swings,
Candy and things
Must come true.

We sit to eat breakfast
Even then he stares at me
He knows I'll be with him all day
No work
Just play

Beautiful bright skies
Accentuated by the
Warm sun
That seems to only
Be shining
On his swing.
We get ice cream and candy
Which makes his eyes large and bright
Taking my eyes
Off his wide handsome smile
For just a moment.

We go home hand in hand
Neither one of us
Wanting to let go
He stays with me
As I clean up and
Get ready for dinner
He helps me and
Never leaves my side

And when we sit down
For dinner
He looks like an angel
Untouched
He sounds like one too
Soft-spoken
But he doesn't want me
To feed him
He won't let me clean him
Instead
He
Picks up the fork,
Feeds himself
And smiles at me.

When it's time to sleep
I sit down next to his
Tired body,
Stroke his face,
And quietly make the promises
That just like this morning,
He'll remember when he
Wakes up tomorrow.

It was in the hospital
That while still only a day old

Lying in a bassinet
He with his big beautiful brown eyes
Noticeably outlined by his
Long, lustrous
Eyelashes
And soft, sweet-smelling
Puerto Rican skin
Captured my heart.

My family surrounded us
Yet he stared up at me
I knew from that moment
Just how it would be
Yet now
He seems so grown
But he is only two.

Jessica Roman *Bronx, New York*

As We Sit Here

As we sit here
Nothing to do
Nancy in the corner swinging her quilt
Joan, Elizabeth and I playing dominoes
The night is still
The air is dry
The fire burning, as we sit here
Our surroundings are damaged
And our cupboard is bare
It is another night with nothing
To do
As we sit here time is ticking
The fire is burning
And I can smell the sweet of
Elizabeth's pipe
Strong, sweet and relaxing
But soon it will be time to go
The little ragged door in the corner
Will be our way out

Dayvie Paschall *Washington, D.C.*

Why Do They Say

What is it, why do they say,
When I was your age I had
To walk ten miles to school,
You could get five king-size candy bars
For a nickel, I learned to swim
When I was five, I had a job when
I was nine, it was so safe you
Didn't have to lock your doors.
We couldn't walk ten feet away
From the porch. Why do they
Say when I was your
Age I was just like
You.

Armand *San Francisco*

Chisme / Gossip

There's this *chisme* about my grandma and grandpa,
Before my mother and all of her brothers and sisters were
    born.
Somebody told my aunts and uncles
And I've heard them talking about it
When this cousin from L.A. visits.
What I've heard is that my grandpa had a big crush on
    my grandma,
But my grandma had this boyfriend and she hated my
    grandpa.
Supposedly, my grandpa had to do something
So that my grandma would fall in love with him.
My family says that my grandpa found this witchcraft
    book
Near some tree and that he was doing all these weird
    things with it.
I've asked my family, "What did he do? Did he drink
    something?
Did he make her drink something?"
But they didn't know or wouldn't tell me.
Anyway, I think my grandpa gave her some kind of herb
    thing.
And just like that, my grandma dumped the other guy
And went running to my grandpa's arms.

Dalia Citlali Garcia Mantanez *San Francisco*

No Gumbo for Me

The first time I had gumbo
I thought it would be nasty,
But my grandmother said,
"It's good."

I was five years old.
I didn't really know
What she was talking about.

I said,
"I don't want that.
It stinks."

My grandma said,
"My gumbo does not stink."

So I had some from my grandpa's bowl.
It was so good.

I told my grandma,
"Sorry,"
Because I really did like it.

So I asked her,
"Can I have some more?"
She said,
"Yes, you can,
Miss Smart Mouth."

Paulesha Pulliam *San Francisco*

Nani

She is the bright orange,
Orange as the evening sun.
She smells like the early morning breeze.
She is the soft cloud of clattering dishes
When they are being washed.
She moves slowly through the long, narrow balcony,
One step carefully at a time.
She sits by the window reading the Koran
With her cat, Manju, next to her,
Brushing her fur through Nani's feet.
She wears a thin white *salwar kamiz*
With tiny blue flowers and lacy lace,
Plain white pants with a nylon *ordni*
That goes on her head, loops around her neck
With the end hanging down her chest.
Her feet are covered with thin rubber *chappals*
That clap against her feet each time she walks.
She has a tiny purse with crisp rupees and coins
And the key to the house that she tucks in her bra strap
With a pink handkerchief called a *ramal*.
In her nose, she wears a big flowerlike nose pin
With red and white rubies
She dreams about the day

That we will come back from school in Bombay,
Where I live with my parents and other grandma.
She dreams about filling
The basketlike jars that hang from the ceiling
With freshly made butter biscuits
Bought from the store by the river.
She will say, *"Jali gahri aha,"*
Come home early.

Asefa Subedar *San Francisco*

My Hands Are Like Sparrows

"My hands are like sparrows," she said
No one would listen
"They feel like stars caught in a tangled
dance of branches"
The girl without a name was very dramatic and poetic
Whenever her hands were dirty
She would say that her hands
Were like sparrows because they
Were so black
They felt like stars caught in a tangled dance
Of branches because they were so sticky
And all her mother would say is
Don't touch the walls

Randall Jackson *Washington, D.C.*

Someone Taught Me

Someone taught me
Right from wrong taught me that
Having sex at a young age is wrong
That I'm not gonna have any self-
Respect for myself that trying to be
Grown-up takes away from my childhood
And pride losing your virginity and wearing
Tampons instead of pads carrying
A child for 9 months would wait
For later life, think about the better
Things in life than crying about boys
And worrying about sex be who
You are instead of who you're not.

Sarah Lydia Chaleman *Bronx, New York*

furious

"A word once let out of the cage cannot be
whistled back again."

—Horace

Think of a range of emotions that you might go through in a day.

Find concrete images that describe these invisible feelings.

Furious

My name is furious
I live in the House of Darkness
My favorite game is Truth, Dare, or Consequences
You better tell the truth
You better do my dare
Or you will suffer the consequences
My favorite color of lipstick is
The darkest shade of burgundy
My eyes are full of fire
My mouth is full of heartbreaking words
My heart is full of ice and stone
My hands are like bricks
My eyebrows are your warning
Don't talk if they say no
Do if they say so
My favorite food is burnt lasagna
Because the world is
Black, bloody and cheesy to me anyway
I drive a purple car, but I love walking
In the valley of the shadow of death
Because I am furious.

Karen Baylor *Washington, D.C.*

Alone

Alone is a darkness that laughs in your face.
When you wake up it will all be erased.
You think you're safe
Ha, please the treatment gets done by everybody
      even me.
I have been scared and sometimes shed a few tears
Lying down in my cold bed thinking it's not real.
My eyes almost closed, brain half asleep, mine in
Wonderland it must be the heat.
Now I want to go to bed and
Now I am beneath Alone's wing.

Christine Rich *Bronx, New York*

I Lost Myself

I have lost myself in the cold wind of
November
I have been stripped of my sanity and
Left lying bare on the sidewalk
My past is a haunting memory
And like all memories it comes and goes
As it pleases
Occasionally to tease
Mostly to torture
And sometimes
Just sometimes it'll bring back a piece of me
Whispering a sweet murmur of he
He who I used to be
I have lost myself
I thought I remembered leaving it next to
My keys on the desk beside my bed so
I wouldn't forget it
It must have burned with the rest of my home
I think it must have panicked
After seeing the smoke consume its world
And it ran, ran as fast as it could
Hoping the flames wouldn't catch him
I saw myself running, running fast

Running past me
I told it how much I missed it
But it was moving faster than the
Speed of sound
Hoping the flames wouldn't catch him

Beside the Shore

Away from civilization, the hurt and the pain
There I lay beside the shore.

Where seagulls fly, and the ocean floats quietly by
There I lay beside the shore.

Watching dolphins swim and listening to the
Moaning of the wind
There I lay beside the shore.

Away from civilization, the hurt and the pain
There I lay beside the shore.

Davon Smith *Washington, D.C.*

Anger That Lives Upon Us

Anger wears a jacket
Of hottest flames.

The color
Of the flames is blue. Touch it

And you'll be burned.
Not your body but your mind

Until you can't think
Only hate.

Anger lives in a dark place
So no one will bother him.

Lawrence Agbayani *San Francisco*

Untitled

Feeling depressed is like
A rainy day because it's
Cold and dark
Feeling brain-dead is like
The color white because
Everything is a blank
Pain is like an animal

Marlene Sanchez *San Francisco*

The Anger Inside Me

When the anger inside me is shown,
You start to moan and groan.
Why does she have to act this way, you say?
Someone else says, "Oh, maybe she's having a bad day."
The day doesn't have to do with the way I act.
But the way you're acting, you just might get smacked.
I walk away, not paying attention to you.
Then you act like a big person and your little friends
    start to laugh and coo
But don't worry, because they'll soon get smacked too.

Sometimes I imagine the beast within me.
Is it a white tiger, or a gray wolf, I can't see.
But if I had to choose, that's what it would be.

Have you ever seen me cry, and if you're lucky act shy?
I know I act tough and try to hang out with the guys.
But they don't want a girl around.
They try to act cool and tell me not to make a sound.
All I do is stand there and stare.
The way they talk, it seems like I'm not even here.
Not even here, far away in space . . .
But that's not how I am, and that's not the case.

The anger inside me seems like a spreading fire.
You are the one that starts it, you liar.
Ongoing, everlasting, spreading by the minute.
But the biggest fire, my heart, don't try to win it.
Because you won't like that beast within me, whatever
It may be.

Amena Dean *Bronx, New York*

Would You Leave Me Too?

We fear ordinary
We feel extraordinary
Cause of hell
My head sailed, my body is dead as well
My soul led by death
My heart burn to crust
My art turn to rust
My body peels
My arms move like wheels
Would you leave me too?

Death is my reward
My legs are drained tubes
My eggs that hatched are cats and crows
To heal the earth
My tears are seeds
My mind it speeds
From dusk to dawn
Death takes cupid beyond
Would you leave me too?

To my mistakes, the jimmy jakes
Can you destroy my mind?

Can you destroy my kindness?
Despite your thoughts!
Forget your thoughts!
Would you leave me too?

I'm deadly, deadly, deadly
I'm soulless, soulless, soulless
I'm ready, ready, ready
WOULD YOU LEAVE ME TOO?

Joseph Roldan *Bronx, New York*

Rant

I remember when my first crush died of a
Drive-by.
I remember when I felt like the whole world
Stopped.
I remember when his death was announced
On all the TV news, and on the front page
Of all the newspapers.
I remember when I swore to God that I would
Never get involved in gangs.
I remember when I saw him in his coffin.
I am sick of all the gangsters in crime.
I've had it with all the young boys and girls
Getting into something, and not know what
Things are all about.
Don't tell me to get jumped into nothing.
I am not your little follower.
I don't want to die before my time.
I am not a sellout.
Don't call me one just because I have my
Head on straight, and know what's wrong
And what's not.
Don't ever ask me to change my mind.

Mirna Franco *San Francisco*

Hard Candy

I'm the broken pieces on the floor.
Some people see me, some people just ignore.
And it just goes by.

I'm cold in the wind and there's a fire in a box
But I can't get the key because I'm lost.
I'm the broken pieces on the floor.

I'm a crank with a missing gear,
But I will be fixed some day, some month, some year.
And it just goes by.

I'm the person that needs a helping hand,
But instead you atomize my thoughts.
I'm the broken pieces on the floor.

It is the color of an eclipse, black,
And I can't see it right in front of me.
And it just goes by.

Don't go nowhere, but they know I'm there
In the cracks of hard bitter life.
I'm the broken pieces on the floor.
And it just goes by.

Craig *San Francisco*

The Tree That's in Front of My House

> "Go inside yourself. Discover the motive that bids you write; examine whether it sends its roots down to the deepest places of your heart, confess to yourself whether you would have to die if writing were denied you. This before all: ask yourself in the quietest hour of your night: must *I* write?"
>
> —Rainer Maria Rilke

The Poetry Circle

**With a group of friends, create a circle within which you can
read your poetry to each other. These are the rules:**

- Everyone in the circle is equal.
- No one's voice is more important than any one else's.
- Everyone in the circle is a teacher.
- Everyone in the circle is a student.
- Everyone has his or her turn to speak within the circle.
- When one is speaking, all others listen.
- The circle is sacred and special.

Living in My Elevator

If I were trapped in an elevator
I'd build a phone out of shoelaces and
Quarters
And call the furniture store
I'd play with all the buttons
And do a cartwheel
I'd check my pulse
And go bungee jumping
With no bungee
I'd wish I had a TV
But

All and all
It's much better than my room
As I take a look around
I realize there's no one in this
Rectangular box
Fall on the phone and squirm like a
Ringworm
I'd turn off the lights
And stare at my hands
And if someone finds me
I'd ask them to close the door

And tell them
"This is a private conference, do you
mind!"
It seems everyone cares if you are trying to get
Out of an elevator
But nobody cares if you are trying
To stay In

Jessica Rawls *Washington, D.C.*

The Spring in Your Voice

The spring voice sounds smooth
In your voice.
It makes you talk as the spring breeze
Goes flying toward a world of no end.
Voices are appearing from the
Spring of no end.
From the den of a bear to the voice
Of your spirit.
You will find a never-lasting wind
In that spirit.
When the bears come out for spring
It has a voice saying welcome to the new world.
It makes you think of spring
In the voice of your spirit flying in the air
The spring in your voice.

Jessica Diaz *Bronx, New York*

My City

If you came to my city,
You wouldn't hear
A robin chirping
As she nests in the trees.
You would hear
The wild, tangled coos
Of furious pigeons fighting
Over a hard piece of bread.

If you came to my city,
You wouldn't hear
The sound of silence
In the morning.
You would hear car horns,
People yelling, dogs barking,
And the occasional
Cat screech.

Yep, my city
Is noisy, loud and unfair,
But it's my home
And what I grew up with.

Though it may be tough,
Mean and hard
It will always be
My city.

Reina Samuels *Washington, D.C.*

On U Street It Sounds Like

On U Street it sounds like
A football game every day
But on Sunday it feels like
A nice day in the park
But at my house it feels
Like a big ship
Like the *Titanic*
On the day it sailed
It tastes like salt

Ricky Wright *Washington, D.C.*

Red Cross

There she is
Ms. Fisher on the steps of the Red Cross
She sleeps there, you know
"The dog who jumps in the sea loses his bone!" she
    shouts
We laugh, my friends and I, and swiftly walk by
I notice a tear form in the crack of her eye
I went to her one day at the steps of the Red Cross
She sleeps there, you know
The day after she smelled of shoes
The skin of her face looked as if it were peeled, dried or
    fried around her cheeks
Probably from crying
Crying, she pulled me down and whispered in my ear
"When a butterfly is pinned down a stream of time
    stops"
I closed my eyes and shuddered because her breath
    smelled like moldy
Porkchops
I smiled
Gave her a dollar
And left.
I went home and asked my mother about the woman
    always on the steps of the

Red Cross

She sleeps there, you know

She said her name was Vanessa

I thought to myself that Vanessa means butterfly

I heard she was crazy, my mom said

I ran upstairs and called the police,

"There's a woman on the steps of the Red Cross

She sleeps there, you know"

The police went

They looked

She was asleep to the point where she couldn't open her
    eyes

It surprised me

Vanessa Fisher

"When a butterfly is pinned down . . ."

Her stream of time stopped.

Spring Haiku

The springtime river
Flows as far as waves and tides
Like blue lions running.

The sky blue water
Runs deep in the ocean floor
Forever like fish.

The seas of the world
Rise high like the blue rainbow
And fall like river.

The sea is dancing
But the ocean is singing.
The river is listening.

Springtime is coming
Dancing butterfly and bird
The springtime queen sings.

Phu Pham *Washington, D.C.*

D'Ark

She is always there
Sitting upon her horse
Head toward the sun
Like a saint
She has been there long
Rusty, tired and dirty
Yet she waits
Like a peacock on a mission
She wants to leave, she cannot
The plague beneath binds her to the ground
So she sits
In a shell
Attached to a metal horse

She ponders her surroundings
Eyes to the sun though she wants to look away
She cannot
Her neck is stiff and hard as her hopes
So she prays for a miracle a sign or at least
Relief from her burden
Hand raised with only the hilt of a sword
The blade left long ago
The war is over

You don't have to fight
You don't have to suffer
You don't have to stand like a statue to be noticed
People can see
You have come to rest and overlook this view
To hear the murmur of trees and the humming of bees
You have come for another chance
To listen
Listen
Listen to the statue that doesn't speak
But tells a story.

Isaac Colon III *Washington, D.C.*

The Tree That's in Front of My House

There's a brown tree in front of my house
With no leaves, only with the long, long branches
Every spring I want for it to blossom
But it never does
But still I write an ode to it because
In a long, long city street
It is the only tree
I take a chair outside every spring afternoon
I sit under it even though it doesn't cover
The sun in my face
I sit there and read a book
And the smell of the branches
Of the tree that is in front of my house
Takes me to a park
Away from my long, boring
City street

Evelyn Canales *Washington, D.C.*

What Does the Ocean Dream of in Its Secret Heart?

Ocean dreams of sun and birds.

Ocean
dreams of water,
                    rain
            and skyline.

Ocean dreams of summer,
            sunflowers
                        and fog.

I dream of you
and I
sitting
            in the middle of a field
        between flowers.

Sahana Rangooni *San Francisco*

I Am . . .

I am the little fire in the grasslands.
I am the little star in the sky.
I am the little cloud flying in the evening.
I am . . .

I am the Golden Gate Bridge standing in the bay.
I am the space shuttle flying in the space.
I am the Great Wall sleeping on the land.
I am . . .

Qishu Hu *San Francisco*

Scene in Tibet

The horses
Are lying down
Beneath the mountain.

Two people are cooking
On the ground
Over a wood fire.

They have killed a buffalo
With a knife
And taken off its skin
To clean and sell
The meat.

Jay Luo *San Francisco*

Leaving China

To say good-bye
Words sick at my heart
My tears would not drop out.

Jia Hua Miao *San Francisco*

What's in a Minute

Right now a man sitting on a bench is
Laughing, a woman is giving birth
To a boy in a car, a girl is getting
Caught stealing from a store, birds
Are flying around the park, a
Beetle is crawling on my book,
My brother is out with his
Girlfriend kissing on the bus,
I'm all alone sitting on a bench
Thinking about what to write,
Somebody is running away from
Home, an old lady just got hit
By a truck while trying to cross
The street, a white house is
Burning, a girl fell off the
Monkey bars, somebody
Is committing suicide, a boy
Is getting jumped by three guys,
Somebody is taking a cold
Shower, somebody is eating

Christina Duculan *San Francisco*

Daydream Nation

Let me take you to a place,
Where the sun is bright,
The trees are full
And the animals dancing with me.

Paradise.
Where I escape my fears,
Become free
To dance and sing with the deer.

Dance I say,
Dance!
Sing I say,
Sing!

Can you see yourself with me?
Where my daydream nation begins?
Fly free with me
And feel
The warmth where the sun is bright
And feel
The present where the trees are full
See the beautiful sight when the angels

Appear
And the animals dance with you and me.
Now that's seeing the world from
Beginning to end.
Then never appear to
Reality again

Dance, I say
Dance!
Sing, I say
Sing!

Samantha Dandridge *Washington, D.C.*

WritersCorps History

"I am in love with WritersCorps."
—Robert Hass, U.S. Poet Laureate, 1995–97

Since its inception in 1994, WritersCorps has helped more than 40,000 people in some of America's most economically disadvantaged neighborhoods improve their literacy and self-sufficiency. WritersCorps has transformed the lives of thousands of youth at risk by teaching creative writing, giving voice to young people whose voices have been systematically ignored or disregarded. With its poetry slam league and award-winning publications, WritersCorps has become a national arts and literacy model.

WritersCorps was born out of discussions between Jane Alexander, former Chairman of the National Endowment for the Arts (NEA), and Eli Siegel, then director of AmeriCorps. Today, hundreds of writers have committed to teach in their communities, inspire youth, and work diligently to create a safe place for young people to write and discover themselves in the process. WritersCorps teachers make lasting connections with their community and become valued mentors and role models.

San Francisco, Washington, D.C., and Bronx, N.Y., were selected as the three initial sites for WritersCorps, chosen for their cities' exemplary arts agencies with deep community roots and traditions of community activism among writers. In these three cities, WritersCorps established writers, working at public schools and social service organizations, have helped people of virtually every race, ethnicity and age improve literacy and communication skills, while offering creative expression as an alternative to violence, alcohol and drug abuse.

In 1997, WritersCorps made the transition from a federally funded program to an independent alliance, supported by a collaboration of public and private partners. DC WritersCorps, Inc., is now a nonprofit organization while the San Francisco and Bronx WritersCorps are projects of the San Francisco Arts Commission and Bronx Council for the Arts, respectively. WritersCorps has developed a national structure administered by the three sites to provide greater cooperation and visibility, while at the same time allowing the independence for each site to respond most effectively to its community.

To learn more about WritersCorps contact:
Bronx WritersCorps: 718-409-1265 or www.bronxarts.org
DC WritersCorps: 202-332-5455 or www.dcwriterscorps.org
San Francisco WritersCorps: 415-252-4655
or www.writerscorps-sf.org